CW00429976

LEYTON & LEYTONSTONE PAST & PRESENT

ALAN SIMPSON

Leyton Parish Church.

Frontispiece: The new sorting office in Fillebrook Road, Leytonstone, soon after opening in 1912. In 1917, Leytonstone became the London E11 delivery area and Leyton became London E10. This building was demolished in 1992 to make way for the A12 (M11 Link Road).

Left: Leyton parish church, *c.* 1905. One of the curates of Leyton parish, Thomas Bowdler, who worked here around 1803, achieved notoriety as the expurgator of Shakespeare's plays and saw his name move into the English language as a result.

First published 2009
Reprinted 2012, 2013

The History Press
The Mill, Brimscombe Port
Stroud, Gloucestershire, GL5 2QG
www.thehistorypress.co.uk

© Alan Simpson, 2009

The right of Alan Simpson to be identified as the Author of this work has been asserted in accordance with the Copyrights, Designs and Patents Act 1988.

British Library Cataloguing in Publication Data.
A catalogue record for this book is available from the British Library.

ISBN 978 0 7524 4931 9

Typesetting and origination by The History Press
Printed in Great Britain

CONTENTS

ACKNOWLEDGEMENTS

I would especially like to thank the following for their generosity and help in completing this book: Satvinder Riyat for the loan of several postcards and photographs from his amazing collection; David Boote for permission to reproduce some of his Waltham Forest Civic Trust photographs, and for his help in contacting members of the Leyton & Leytonstone Historical Society; and Jo Brown for allowing me to use two of her photographs in this book. I would also like to thank Ruth Jones and my brother, Philip, for walking the streets of Leyton and Leytonstone with me helping to identify locations old and new.

All the modern photographs here were taken by me, mostly in 2008, but a few in 2009. A handful of the older photographs were also taken by me, but the majority of the older views are from postcards or photographs in my own collection or in that of Satvinder Riyat. In some cases it has not been possible to identify the copyright owners, so I apologise if I have unintentionally infringed upon anyone's copyright.

I would also like to acknowledge here the use that I have made of information in the *Victoria County History of Essex*. Volume 6 covers the Leyton and Leytonstone area and is a valuable resource for local historians.

If this book stirs your interest in local history and you would like to donate photographs to be added to the London Borough of Waltham Forest's historical collections, or lend original photographs for copying, please contact the curator at Vestry House Museum, Vestry Road, Walthamstow, London, E17 9NH. Tel. 020 84964391. Email vhm.enquiries@walthamforest.gov.uk.

INTRODUCTION

Leyton lies about six miles north-east of central London between the River Thames and Epping Forest. The town, including Leytonstone, became an Urban District in 1895 and was incorporated as a Borough in 1926. It lost its independence in 1965 when it was merged with Walthamstow and Chingford to become the London Borough of Waltham Forest. The area is mainly a dormitory suburb of small houses built between 1870 and 1910, interspersed with modern block- and tower-housing. Leyton is fortunate in having within its borders large tracts of open land. The north-east corner, known as Whipps Cross, includes over 200 acres of Epping Forest, while abutting on to Leytonstone in the south-east are Wanstead Flats. In the west is Leyton Marsh through which the River Lea, forming the western boundary of the borough, flows on its way to the Thames.

Many years ago, Leyton and Leytonstone were quite separate villages. Eighteenth-century maps show what are now High Road Leyton and High Road Leytonstone as the principle roads, with Lea Bridge Road becoming a main highway after the building of the first road bridge in 1757. Small settlements grew up at Harrow Green, the Green Man, Knotts Green and Whipps Cross. By this time, as Philip Morant observed, the area had become a 'pretty retiring place from London' for wealthy merchants, bankers and professional men. They built fine houses or rebuilt existing ones, and established large households. In 1766 some fifty to sixty gentlemen's families were living in the parish along with several black servants from the Indies. In Leyton, about a quarter of a mile west of the High Road stood the parish church with the manor house of Leyton Grange beside it.

Leyton and Leytonstone remained rural until the mid-nineteenth century. Before the coming of the railway the main occupations were agricultural or market gardening. Leyton Marsh had been common farming land since the Middle Ages. Grazing rights on the marshes belonged to all the inhabitants from 1 August (Lammas Day) until 25 March (Lady Day) of each year. The opening of railways to London, with stations at Lea Bridge, Leyton and Leytonstone was followed by the provision of cheap and speedy transport. This coincided with the expansion of opportunities for employment in offices and in industry in London and in neighbouring districts. By the end of the nineteenth century the effect was to transform the two villages into a suburban dormitory for clerks and workmen, mostly employed outside the area. The pull towards living in the area was not created by a local demand for labour; this was never a centre of manufacturing such as Stratford or West Ham. The vast majority of wage-earners, artisans and clerks made their daily way towards the City.

When the Eastern Counties Railway arrived, a letter published in *The Times* on 23 April 1857 reported that since the line had opened '...mouldy mansions at Wanstead and Woodford, Leytonstone and Loughton were furnished up, and avidly taken by the brokers and others; house property along the line rose by 20% in value... season tickets were taken up to an unexpected amount, and an extraordinary number of daily passengers went regularly up and down, so that this branch, with a prosperity unparalleled in ECR annals actually paid more than had been calculated on'.

House-building on a substantial scale began in earnest in the 1870s, and gathered momentum as the century drew to a close. The development of Leyton was accomplished steadily, though piecemeal, as estates were brought on to the market. Once speculative development had begun, Leyton ceased to attract wealthy residents in search of rural seclusion. Early estates to be developed were Grange Park (1860); Holloway Down (1867) developed around the Union Workhouse, which became Langthorne Hospital; Fillebrook (1870s) and Ruckholt Manor (1860s). The Midland Railway's route across the area in 1894 meant that housing development would continue. A parish that had a population figure in 1861 of just 4,794 would by 1901 be an Urban District of 98,912 people. The days of the great houses established here in the eighteenth century were effectively over and although some buildings survived for a while as schools or asylums, few lasted for long.

The new houses were mainly yellow-brick two-storey terraces and villas, ranged in rows, their bow-windows and doorways freely ornamented with mass-produced cement foliage and tracery. Retail shops, which became increasingly necessary for the growing population, were almost entirely confined to the main thoroughfares, long stretches of which were built up as shopping streets in the later nineteenth century. The new frontages were of two or three storeys with shops on the ground floor and living accommodation for their owners above. Later, as demand grew, residential terraces were brought into use, with shops built over their small front gardens. The main land development companies in Leyton were the Freehold Land Society and the British Land Company, as well as the Warner Estates. No Victorian or Edwardian mansions were built in the area as it had ceased to have a rural feel, and by 1909–11, the council was trying to restore the ambience of 'leafy Leyton' by putting unemployed men to work planting thousands of street trees.

During the First World War about 1,300 houses in Leyton and Leytonstone were damaged by bombing during the Zeppelin raids. During the Second World War, hardly a house escaped damage. There was little building between the two wars, and after 1945 municipal redevelopment began on vacant and cleared sites. It was not until the late 1950s and early 1960s that most of the large housing estates were begun. First, schemes provided houses and bungalows of conventional design or three- and four-storey blocks of flats. By the 1960s, the council was building upward at higher densities. Like elsewhere in the country, the tower blocks rose and were seen as the solution to mass housing shortages. Some of these tower blocks have now been demolished and more community-minded low-level housing constructed.

Since the 1950s the area covered by Waltham Forest today has become a popular place for many people who emigrated to Britain, especially from the Caribbean, India and Pakistan. Now over a quarter of the population of Waltham Forest belongs to the ethnic communities, and the borough has the second-largest Pakistani population in Britain.

Pictorial history, as a popular source of information, reveals architectural, transport, fashion and social trends. Many people enjoy looking at old postcards and photographs as they bring back memories and highlight changes. Many changes have occurred in Leyton and Leytonstone over the years, and whilst the majority of the following pictures represent the early part of the twentieth century, the more recent 'past' photographs also show what has changed within the last thirty years.

Our journey through Leyton and Leytonstone begins at Lea Bridge Road, takes us down High Road Leyton and then up High Road Leytonstone to the Green Man. We then travel along Church Lane and into the Fillebrook and Bushwood areas, before finally heading off to Whipps Cross.

1

LEA BRIDGE ROAD

LEYTON, LEABRIDGE ROAD   73381

Lea Bridge Road, looking in the direction of Whipps Cross from the Bakers Arms,
c. 1935. The Bakers Arms is a busy crossroads where Lea Bridge Road, Hoe Street and
High Road Leyton all meet. Here, a London Transport tram on route 61 heads for Clapton.
The Bakers Arms area had a wide variety of shops over the years, including lots of fruit
and vegetable stores, furniture shops and little clothes shops. There also used to be a
Manzies pie and mash shop where one could view live eels crawling around an ice block.

Lea Bridge station, *c.* 1910. The station was opened on 18 September 1840 when the line from Stratford to Broxbourne was built by the Northern & Eastern Railway. For the first year, the station was named Lea Bridge Road. The building was designed by the architect Sancton Wood and had a bell turret on the roof. In this once hung a bell which was rung to warn intended passengers of the approach of trains timed to call at the station. A staircase on each side of the booking hall led to the platforms and the arches at the bottom of the steps served as waiting rooms. The street-level building was damaged by fire on 31 March 1944, and subsequently partially demolished. Its remains continued to stand for a number of years afterwards, but they were eventually replaced with a new structure of modern design. Goods services were withdrawn from the station on 7 December 1970 and the station closed completely on 8 July 1985. The modern structure at street level remains behind the advertising hoardings, but it is now reduced to a glassless shell.

Lea Bridge Road, by Lea Bridge station, 19 December 1944. To the east of Lea Bridge station was the Signals & Telegraph Department building of the Great Eastern Railway; this had its own siding with a sharply curved spur line that included a demonstration signal box. All this was demolished when a parcels depot was built on the site in 1939. In December 1944 the depot was struck by a flying bomb and the result is apparent in the photograph. It was during the Second World War that the heart of Lea Bridge station was destroyed, for although the frontage survived, the building was gutted by fire, not by enemy action, on 31 March 1944. The gaunt remains of the station are visible on the bridge in the December murk. Modern-day road improvements have led to the construction of Argall Way through the site of the former parcels depot beyond the factory in the modern photograph.

Lea Bridge Road, at the junction with Markhouse Road and Church Road, *c.* 1960. In the early twentieth century Lea Bridge Road was a cobbled road with tram tracks all the way, and a speed limit for buses and motor cars of 12mph. The cobblestones were laid around the tram tracks, but on each side, before tarmac came about, there were wood blocks. The road was widened on several occasions and the cobblestones were eventually removed. The cinema visible at the right-hand side of the photograph opened as the Savoy on Boxing Day 1928. It was the first local cinema to have 'talkies'; Al Jolson in *The Singing Fool* was shown there on 24 June 1929. The Savoy had become the Odeon by the time of this photograph. The building survives, but it is now a bingo hall.

Lea Bridge Road in the 1950s. An *Official Guide to Leyton* from the mid-1930s records that extraordinary developments with regard to shopping had taken place, particularly in the area that surrounded the Savoy cinema in Lea Bridge Road. There, from a nucleus of small but well-equipped shops, had grown up a centre which bid fair to rival the town's main shopping centres. One such example was the Broadway Market, a modern range of small shops opened in 1934. Early occupants included a fishmonger and a greengrocer. The building survives, and it now houses the likes of an internet café and a motor parts specialist.

The Bakers Arms, *c.* 1910. Formerly known as Leyton Corner, this locality shares the identity of its public house, which was named in honour of the nearby almshouses built in 1857 by the London Master Bakers' Benevolent Institution. In 1883, a horse tram line was laid through Bakers Arms from Lea Bridge to Whipps Cross, but it was an abortive attempt at public transport. In 1889, a successful tramway was opened and extended to the Rising Sun (an inn a little beyond Whipps Cross), and three years later across the Lea Bridge to Clapton. In 1906, the tramway was electrified by Leyton Council. A Leyton tram on the Clapton run can be seen crossing the newly electrified junction.

2

HIGH ROAD LEYTON

High Road Leyton, looking north to the junction with Church Road, *c.* 1910. On the left is the Lido Picture Palace, which later became home to the Leyton and Leytonstone Club & Institute. The house beyond the junction is Leyton's vicarage, dating from 1893. This was sold to Leyton Council in 1958 and was demolished in 1959. In 1961, a block of flats named John Strype Court was completed on the site. John Strype was one of the most notable incumbents of the parish, being both a noted antiquarian and vicar of Leyton from 1669–1737.

Livingstone College, c. 1907. Originally known as Knotts Green House, Livingstone College was built in 1786 for Gilbert Slater, an East India merchant. In 1821, the house was purchased by the Barclay family, the founders of Barclays Bank, and became Barclay House. Robert Barclay lived there from 1821–53 and his son, Joseph Gurney Barclay, from 1853–98. By 1898, when Joseph Gurney Barclay died, the estate covered 100 acres. In that year the estate was auctioned and, with the exception of the house and two and a half acres of grounds, sold for development. In 1900, the house became Livingstone Medical College for Missionaries. In both World Wars, Livingstone College was adapted to serve as a hospital. In 1947, the college moved to Reigate. The house remained empty until 1951 when it was acquired by Leyton Council. In 1952, Livingstone Court flats were built in the grounds. The house itself, leased as offices for a few years after 1954, was demolished in 1961. A block of flats called Livingstone College Towers was built on the site in 1963. This seventeen-storey tower block was demolished in 1995 and has been replaced by modern low-rise housing.

Kings Hall, High Road Leyton, *c.* 1910. Two principal north-south roads ran through the parish of Leyton. One of these was High Road Leyton (originally named Church Street) off which the village centre of Low Leyton developed. In the early years of the twentieth century, several cinemas were opened in the area, some in purpose-built buildings, and others in converted buildings. The Kings Hall, on the corner of High Road Leyton and Belmont Park Road, became the Kings cinema, later renamed the Century cinema. By 1976, the building had become a supermarket. The newer entrance to the former cinema survives today, but shops have been built on much of the site of the old Kings Hall.

High Road Leyton, *c.* 1990. The austere 1930s brick building to the right of the photograph was originally the Electric Showrooms. During the Second World War it was transformed into the first of two British Restaurants opened in Leyton by the National Coalition government to supply hot meals at a reasonable price, especially useful for those who had suffered in the Blitz. This opened in March 1942 and had seating for 250 and served 1,500 main meals per week. Leyton swimming baths were almost next door. They opened in 1934 and were demolished in the 1990s to be replaced by the Leyton Leisure Lagoon further down the High Road. The small tiled building to the left of the photograph was all that was left of the 1934 baths. This, and the two-storey eighteenth-century building next door, were subsequently swept away and replaced by a new shopping parade. The British Restaurant building remains as a Cash Converters shop.

Leyton Green, with the Post Office and newsagent on the left, *c*. 1905. A V1 flying bomb landed at Leyton Green in 1944, causing widespread damage. An open-air market was held on the site until it was redeveloped as Market Parade in 1962–63. Leyton Green Towers, an eleven-storey tower block, was completed in 1963. Leyton Green Road, leaving the right-hand side of the photograph, was the site of the White House, a seventeenth-century building demolished before the Second World War. The Great Eastern London Motor Omnibus Company built a bus garage at Leyton Green in 1906 when a new service was started from the Bakers Arms to Oxford Circus via Lea Bridge Road. The London General Omnibus Company took over the Great Eastern in 1911, and rebuilt and enlarged the Leyton Green depot in 1912.

High Road Leyton, *c.* 1907. One of the Great Eastern London Motor Omnibus Company's buses passing the parade of shops just north of the railway bridge over the High Road by Leyton's Midland Railway station. The railway line had been opened as part of the Tottenham & Forest Gate Railway on 9 July 1894. This six-mile line was a link between the Tottenham & Hampstead Junction Railway and the London, Tilbury & Southend Railway, and was jointly promoted with the Midland Railway. The line was a very late arrival, being built across rapidly developing suburbs, and was difficult and expensive to build. Much of it is on a brick viaduct and it crosses many roads. The tower of the Wesleyan church is visible above the shop roofs. A message on the back of the card reads, 'This is the new motor bus same as I fell off. They are just fine to ride in. You can go from Leyton to Oxford Circus in an hour'.

Wesleyan Church and School. Leyton

'rinted in Germany. T. Hubbard & Son, Hubbard's Corner, Leyton, E.

The Wesleyan church and school, *c.* 1905. Properly known as the Mary Fletcher Memorial church, this church was built in 1877 on the corner of High Road Leyton and James Lane. Designed in an elaborate Gothic style by G. Marshall and built of Kentish rag and Bath stone, it consisted of a nave, with apse and west gallery, supported by pinnacled buttresses. There was a turret over the west entrance, formed by four arches on columns. Temporary iron schoolrooms were built nearby in 1892 and 1894. A permanent Sunday school, matching the church in design, was opened in 1902 – the new, clean building to the left of the church. The church closed in 1969 and it and the Sunday school were demolished in 1971; the site is now occupied by a petrol filling station and small supermarket. That part of James Lane has been renamed Fletcher Lane.

Leyton Midland Road station in the 1950s. The station opened on 9 July 1894 and
was simply named Leyton until 1 May 1949. It is built on a viaduct, widened here to
accommodate the platforms, although the buildings were bracketed out from the sides and
supported by cast-iron columns. These buildings were at the London end of the platforms,
constructed from the standard pattern of wooden prefabricated panels of typical Midland
Railway appearance. Awnings were provided over the platforms for the length of the
buildings. Covered staircases led down the side of the viaduct to street level, connecting
with the wings of the booking hall which was situated in one of the arches of the viaduct,
with its entrance in Midland Road. The station was rationalised in 1971 when the platform
buildings were removed and replaced with brick shelters. When rebuilt, it retained its
original booking office, but the station was later provided with a modern brick-built booking
office of modest proportions. This was subsequently closed at the end of the 1990s and a
new entrance was opened on the up side leading directly onto Leyton High Road. In 2007,
the station became part of the London Overground network, passing into ownership of
Transport for London.

Hainault Road, adjacent to Leyton Midland Road station, *c.* 1910. The cobbled entrance on the right led into the goods and coal yard for Leyton Midland Road station. There was a siding on the up side and the signal box, whilst at the down end of the station, after crossing Hainault Road, the line ran onto a section of embankment and a loop and a further two tracks led down to a head shunt. From this head shunt two sidings led back downwards to the goods and coal yard at ground level. The yard closed in 1968, but the various coal offices facing onto the south-eastern side of Hainault Road were still standing in 1972. They were later demolished and the whole site is now an industrial estate named the Sidings. Nearly all the shops have changed use in the intervening century, but the family chemist at the left survives in the same use, now as the Hainault Pharmacy.

Leyton National School, High Road Leyton, in the 1990s. This school originated in
1816 when Samuel Bosanquet leased a corner of Lawyers' Field in James Lane to
trustees to be used for a school, which was established in 1819. In 1847, the school
united with the Ozler Free School, and a new mixed school was built by subscription
on the Free School site near the Three Blackbirds inn in High Road Leyton – this
is the building in the photograph. By 1874 attendance was increasing rapidly.
Improvements were made, notably in the 1880s. However in the 1890s further
enlargement left the trustees in debt, so in 1900 they transferred the school to the
Leyton School Board. The school, which then became known as High Road School,
was closed in 1903, but re-opened in 1904 as a temporary mixed school. It finally
closed in 1923 and the land and premises were sold around 1925. The building still
existed in 2003 as factories. It has since been demolished and the site may see future
use as part of a new police station.

Leyton Police Station, Francis Road, *c.* 1905. Leyton Police Station was erected on the corner of Francis Road and Morley Road in 1890 and was part of the Metropolitan Police 'J' Division. The Metropolitan Police had been founded in 1829 by the Home Secretary, Sir Robert Peel. The Metropolitan Police Act 1829 defined the original Metropolitan Police District as an area of about seven miles radius from Charing Cross. Within the next year, seventeen police divisions were set up. In 1865, three more divisions were created, and in 1886 'J' Division was added, centred on Bethnal Green. In 1888, just before Leyton police station opened, 'J' Division comprised a superintendent, thirty-eight inspectors, fifty-six sergeants and 522 constables. The station had lodgings above for sixteen men who paid 1*s* a week out of their wages. In 1939, the present station was built on the site. There is talk of a new police station being built around the corner on the site of the old National School.

Essex County Cricket Grounds, Leyton.

Essex County Cricket Ground, High Road Leyton, *c.* 1910. In 1886, the headquarters of Essex County Cricket Club was moved from Brentwood to a more accessible site in High Road Leyton, and a new County Ground was developed there. The new half-timbered pavilion was designed by Richard Creed, and Essex played the inaugural first class match against Leicestershire in 1894. In 1921, the County Ground was sold to the Army Sports Control Board, but continued to be an important venue for County matches. In 1932, the Yorkshire openers Holmes and Sutcliffe made a record-breaking first wicket stand of 555 against Essex on this ground. In 1933, Essex County Cricket Club moved out of the ground, but in 1957 they returned and the ground was used as one of the Essex cricket festival grounds until 1977. In 1999, Waltham Forest Council submitted a Lottery application for funding to restore the pavilion. The restored pavilion is a Grade II listed building and is now the centrepiece of Leyton Youth Centre, which is now based at the ground.

St Mary's church, Leyton, *c.* 1910. The church of St Mary dates from 1658, the principal surviving feature from that date being the red brick tower. The cupola on top of the tower is eighteenth century and was removed from the Great House, Leyton, which stood opposite the cricket ground in the High Road and was demolished in 1905. The extensive alterations that have occurred during the church's long history have added to its picturesque quality. With its atmospheric churchyard and tombstones – some of them listed buildings in their own right, including a notable monument to Samuel Bosanquet by Sir John Soane – the church continues to provide Leyton with a hint of its old village setting. The nearby almshouses also dated from the 1650s. However, these were rebuilt in 1885, with a design by Richard Creed (who also designed the pavilion at the nearby cricket ground) in the Tudor style.

Leyton and Leytonstone Club and Institute, *c.* 1920. The institute was the Leyton and Leytonstone Branch of Comrades of the Great War, an organisation formed in 1917 as a non-political association to represent the rights of ex-service men and women who had served or had been discharged from service during the First World War. Comrades of the Great War was one of the original four ex-service associations that amalgamated in 1921 to form The British Legion. The Institute was in High Road Leyton next door to the Lion & Key Inn, in a building that had earlier been the Lido Picture Palace. By the 1930s, the building was in use as a shirt factory. Today it houses an internet café and a travel agent. On the opposite side of the road stands Grove House. This stands on the site of Cross House, which was rebuilt around 1800 and extended around 1879 when it was renamed Grove House. It remains in use today as Leyton Working Men's Club.

GRANGE ROAD CORNER, LEYTON
A277/1027

Grange Park Road at the junction with High Road Leyton, *c.* 1910. Grange Park Road follows the course of an avenue of trees on the former Grange estate. The Grange itself stood to the north-east of St Mary's church. It was the arrival of the railway in 1856 that saw the demise of the Grange and its estate, which was sold to the British Land Company in 1860. The house was demolished and most of the trees felled in 1861 when the grounds were laid out as building plots, the new estate comprising roughly the district bounded by Park, Church, Vicarage and Thornhill Roads. The buildings on the left of the photograph, including a printers and a dairy, are now the site of flats in Thornhill Gardens. The short post next to the lamppost in the middle of the road was an emergency fire alarm. These were connected to the fire station for use by the public before telephones were commonplace.

Leyton Town Hall, *c.* 1904. This handsome red-brick building with white stone details and a slate roof was designed by John Johnson. It is part of a complex of three adjoining buildings fronting High Road Leyton, Adelaide Road and Ruckholt Road, and was opened by the Duke and Duchess of York on 18 March 1896 as Leyton Council's Public Offices and Technical Institute. The council outgrew this new accommodation within a few years and an extension had to be built in Ruckholt Road in 1910. In 1965, when Leyton became part of the London Borough of Waltham Forest and the new borough's town hall was located in Walthamstow, the building became municipal offices. The building is now listed and plans have been announced for its mixed-use redevelopment.

Leyton Library, *c.* 1904. This gault brick and stone building was originally Leyton's Town Hall. It was designed by John Knight and opened in 1881. However, these earlier public offices soon become inadequate for a borough with the highest rate of population growth of any English town with over 50,000 inhabitants. A new Town Hall was built next door and the old building became a library. This was later refurbished and reopened on 1 September 1929 by the Mayor of Leyton and the poet and playwright John Drinkwater. The building is now listed and it continues to serve as Leyton Library.

Coronation Gardens, *c.* 1925. Coronation Gardens developed from the earlier High Road Recreation Ground. This was a site acquired for open space in 1897, at the time of Queen Victoria's Diamond Jubilee. The Recreation Ground was upgraded to form Coronation Gardens and was opened on 23 May 1903. When the gardens opened they consisted of formally laid out beds, with large areas of grass and a variety of trees and shrubs, and a drinking fountain with metal cups on chains. They soon acquired a bandstand and a children's playground, and on 23 September 1922 the War Memorial Fountain was unveiled by the Lord Lieutenant of Essex. The pillar to the right of the photograph came from the old General Post Office in London. The Memorial Fountain was removed after the Second World War, but as part of the Waltham Forest Millennium celebrations a replacement was erected in the same spot within the Gardens. The Gardens were closed temporarily while the work was carried out and they re-opened in 2003 to commemorate 100 years of this much-loved park in the heart of Leyton.

Great Eastern Railway station, Leyton, *c.* 1910. On 22 August 1856, the Eastern Counties
Railway opened a branch line from Stratford to Woodford and Loughton with stations
at Low Leyton and Leytonstone. The Great Eastern Railway took over the line in 1862,
and dropped the 'Low' from Leyton in 1867. When originally opened, trains were not
allowed to stop at Leyton on Sundays as the vicar had convinced those in authority that
the railway was 'the Devil's work' and they should prevent people from getting to church
by train. In this photograph, a Leyton tram moves away from the stop at Leyton station *en
route* to the Bakers Arms. On the bridge over the railway, next to the coal offices, a West
Ham vehicle descends after having passed another Leyton car heading south.

Leyton station, March 1995. This is the original Eastern Counties Railway station and stationmaster's house, comprising an elegant two-storey building of brown brick with a hipped slate roof. In 1923, the Great Eastern Railway was absorbed into the London and North Eastern Railway (LNER), and in 1933 the London Passenger Transport Board (LPTB) took over responsibility for buses, trams and underground services in the capital. The LPTB produced a report outlining the problems in north-east London with proposals to electrify the LNER suburban lines from Liverpool Street to Shenfield and extend the Central Line in a new tube tunnel from Liverpool Street to Leyton where tube trains would continue at surface level to Loughton and beyond. The coming of the new A12 (M11 Link Road) in the late 1990s, which runs alongside the railway line between Leyton and Leytonstone, required the demolition of the original station building at Leyton and of the secondary entrance there on Langthorne Road.

Great Eastern Railway station, Leyton, c. 1910. A tram pauses at the station before setting off again for Stratford and the Royal Docks. With the subsequent growth in residential traffic, the Great Eastern Railway rebuilt and made improvements at Leyton. In 1888, almost the entire station was reconstructed, including a new main entrance on the High Road bridge, while another exit and entrance was added at the country end in Union (now Langthorne) Road. Progress on extending Central Line services was rapid and by the beginning of 1938 it was anticipated that the Central Line would reach Stratford within two years. However, the Second World War intervened and all work was suspended on 24 May 1940. With the commencement of air attacks on Britain, the westbound tunnel between Leyton and Stratford was used as an air raid shelter, with access from Westdown Road and the High Road. Not until hostilities ceased could the work be completed. At Leyton, a new façade was constructed for the High Road entrance. Electric tube trains finally reached Leyton station on 5 May 1947.

Leyton Civil Engineer's Yard, March 1987. After tube trains reached Leyton in 1947, goods trains continued to run on the line at night, but these were eventually withdrawn. Across the road from the tube station at Leyton lay the former goods yard, which had a small shunting neck. The goods yard closed on 6 May 1968. Alongside the goods yard was the British Rail's Civil Engineer's Yard. This was one of numerous offshoots of the much larger sidings complex at Temple Mills. The Civil Engineers Yard closed in the 1990s and the new A12 (M11 Link Road) was driven through part of its site. The road opened in 1999. The rest of the site was sold by the Department for the Environment, Transport and the Regions with planning permission for retail development and leisure facilities. The supermarket company Asda subsequently teamed up with London & Continental Railways to redevelop the yard as a retail park, which now houses a range of large outlets and is known as Leyton Mills.

Temple Mills marshalling yard, December 1983, looking north from Ruckholt Road over the vast Temple Mills sidings complex. The marshalling yard started life as a goods depot in 1871 and was extended over the years. In 1897, the Great Eastern Railway's wagon department works was moved to Temple Mills (it is just off to the left of the photograph). The wagon works extended over twenty-two acres and were modernised in 1958. The marshalling yard achieved a degree of fame when the climax to the chase at the end of the 1947 film *It Always Rains on Sundays* was filmed there. As part of the 1955 British Railways' Modernisation Plan, the yard underwent a £3.5 million reconstruction. When this was completed in 1958, the marshalling yard, with modern, remote-controlled hump shunting and electronic automatic controls, became not only the largest in Britain but the most up to date in the world. It was closed on 17 May 1993. A depot for diesel locomotives opened on part of the site in 2001, but that had a short life and was demolished in 2008 to make way for the Orient Way carriage sidings. Much of the rest of the site is now home to a maintenance depot for the Eurostar fleet of trains, which cost £402 million and opened in October 2007. The New Spitalfields Market relocated in 1991 from the Old Spitalfields market to the site of the former wagon works.

High Road Leyton, 1960. A view of the southern end of the High Road, near its junction with Frith Road, looking north towards the Central Line railway station. Like much of the High Road, it is lined with shops serving local needs; in 1960 these included a baker and a watchmaker. Half a century later, local needs are for fast food shops, internet access and cheap phone calls. Another significant change is the greatly increased traffic now using the High Road. Deliveries are still made by lorry, although J. Lyons vans no longer deliver Swiss rolls.

3

HIGH ROAD
LEYTONSTONE

Bearmans new arcade, shortly after opening in 1924. Bearmans was founded in 1898
and was Leytonstone's most famous department store – the "Arrods of the East End'.
It was a local institution and a byword for good taste, with an Acorn Club for children,
which entitled them to a tea for two in the restaurant in the basement. Bearmans also
had the greatest Christmas experiences. Going there to visit Father Christmas was
described as magical. A local resident recalls that in one year, children visiting Santa
Claus sat in a large model space ship before arriving in his grotto, in another year they
sat in a sleigh.

The Thatched House pub at the junction of High Road Leytonstone, Crownfield Road and Cann Hall Road in the 1920s. The High Road through Leytonstone was taken over by the Middlesex & Essex Turnpike Trust in 1721, and maintained by the Trust until 1866. The Cannhall turnpike gate was located to the south of the Thatched House pub, which at that time was a little further north than the present one. Alfred Wire, headmaster of a new board school at Harrow Green, recalled that when he came to the district in 1877, Cann Hall Road and Crownfield Road were country lanes. Landlords (or their families) stayed a long time at the Thatched House: between 1826 and 1851 the landlords all came from the Renwick family and between 1896 and 1926 from the Strachan family. By 2008, the pub had closed, but the building survived as the All Seasons café. The Thatched House pub sign was still on display, and the Thatched House continues to feature as a destination on local road signs.

Like the Thatched House (and the Green Man), the Plough & Harrow at Harrow Green is another example of a replacement pub not being built on the original location. A pub named Le Harrow is recorded here back in 1651. The photograph shows a later building in the early years of the twentieth century, and a horse tram passes by on its way to Stratford. This was rebuilt in 1928 on a site immediately to the south. The rebuilt pub is larger, and in more recent years it also saw a brief name change to the Laurel & Hardy. The name has now reverted back to the original. At the beginning of the twentieth century the pub promoted its wide range of beers, wines and spirits; its twenty-first-century counterpart entices people in by showing live football.

HIGH ROAD, LEYTONSTONE   No 3

High Road Leytonstone, opposite the Plough & Harrow pub, *c.* 1920. Just visible beyond the shops on the right is the Academy cinema, which opened on 29 March 1913. This had seating for 650, all on one floor, and the auditorium was set back from and ran parallel to the High Road. The sign outside advertises 'Latest Pictures. Continuous Performance 2 o'c to 10.30. Special reduced prices for matinées'. The shop on the corner of Selby Road displays an impressive array of bicycle wheels, and also has a pump for the sale of Pratts petrol (despite displaying a BP sign above). Of the five shops in that parade in 1920, three had been converted to flats by the early twenty-first century.

The Academy cinema, opposite the Plough & Harrow pub at Harrow Green, in the 1950s. The original Academy cinema closed on 28 August 1933 and was enlarged and given a new modern facade to the plans of architect Frederick Charles Mitchell. The entrance was single-storied and was flanked by shop units on each side. It re-opened as the New Academy Cinema with 1,100 seats on a stadium plan, with a raised section at the rear. In October 1955, it was closed on its purchase by the Granada chain who renamed it the Century when it re-opened. It finally closed as a cinema on 5 January 1963 and was converted into a bingo hall. This in turn closed in July 1983. The building was subsequently demolished and a block of flats known as Paramount House was built on the site.

Harrow Green, *c.* 1905. Over the centuries, the area has rejoiced in a variety of names: Sols Green (1716), Saul's Green (1723), Salls Green (1731) and Salts Green (1777), although it took its present-day name of Harrow Green from the nearby inn called Le Harrow. Harrow Green is officially part of Epping Forest, although it is now in the heart of a built-up area. In 1898, the local newspaper reported that, 'Harrow Green does not justify its name, it is overcrowded with houses, themselves overcrowded; there is absolutely nothing green about it, except in the way of paint'. The solution lay in converting 'an unsightly triangular piece of ground which gives the locality its name, but which is as devoid of greenery as every other part of this ill favoured neighbourhood' into a small public garden. A fountain was constructed in the garden in 1901 and a war memorial was erected in November 1926. Visible on the right is Leytonstone Road Baptist church. This opened in 1902 and was enlarged in 1906. It later became known as the People's Hall. It was gutted by bombing in 1940 and the present building was opened in 1959. It is now the Wesleyan Christian Centre.

Harrow Green, looking north from the junction of Cathall Road and High Road Leytonstone, c. 1910. A writer in 1936 recalled that, 'Seventy years ago, Leytonstone was a village, a beautiful old-world village, stretching from Stratford to the Green Man, a village of cornfields and typical rural surroundings. A toll gate crossed the road near Harrow Green, and my father used to relate how, coming home from Stratford late at night, he aroused the gatekeeper so that he could pass through with his donkey and barrow.' Much development took place in the following years, and overcrowding, combined with poor sanitary conditions, resulted in a death rate greatly above the national average in the 1880s. A smallpox outbreak resulted in ninety-eight cases and twenty-four deaths, mainly at Harrow Green. The baker's shop on the left survives today as a sign shop, but all the buildings on the right were demolished in 1984.

A mid-nineteenth century local directory described Leytonstone as 'a handsome village extending more than a mile along the Stratford and Epping road, to the borders of the Forest, and having many large and handsome houses, with sylvan grounds, mostly occupied as suburban villas by gentlemen of London'. A contemporary writer noted of the High Road that, 'On either side were hedges, and a few old mansions and houses, with large grounds and well-set gardens, generally shut in by large iron-work gates'. Southwell Grove Cottage was typical of those houses. From 1814 to 1836, the house was occupied by Benjamin Nind, a solicitor of Throgmorton Street in the City of London. Southwell Grove Cottage was demolished as the Holloway Down and Park estates were developed in the 1860s and 1870s. Its site is behind the shops facing onto High Road Leytonstone at the junction with Southwell Grove Road. Southwell Grove Road has a small claim to fame as it was hit by bombs from Zeppelin *L10* on 17 August 1915. The Zeppelin bombed a route along the course of the Midland Railway line through the area from Walthamstow to Leyton and Leytonstone. Ten people were killed and forty-eight injured in the raid.

Leytonstone High Road, just north of the Midland Railway bridge, *c.* 1905. The entrance to the station was just beyond the bridge on the right-hand side. Behind the shops on the right lay the goods and coal yard. There was insufficient room between the nearby Great Eastern Railway line and the High Road for the railway tracks to reach the ground level yard, so a wagon hoist had to be installed. On the up side the viaduct was widened to accommodate the platform, whilst on the down side it was widened to take both the platform and a double-track loop which ran behind it, the outermost track of which terminated in the wagon hoist, which was hidden from the High Road by the shops. The goods yard was closed in 1968. The shops were replaced by Panther House, for some time a car showroom, but now a small supermarket and training college. The goods and coal yard is now a large commercial builder's yard.

Leytonstone's Midland Railway station c. 1910. The line was jointly promoted by the Midland Railway and the London, Tilbury & Southend Railway and opened in 1894, with a station at High Road Leytonstone. The up side platform buildings were bracketed from the viaduct, and a covered staircase joined the end of the up platform to the booking hall, which was located in one of the viaduct arches and surrounded by a glazed wooden structure. The down side staircase descended into the viaduct to reach the booking hall. Leytonstone FC had its ground next to the station, and the man standing on the steps looking over the platform wall may well be watching a football match there. The station was renamed Leytonstone High Road station from 1 May 1949. In 1957–58, the station was rebuilt with platform buildings in the contemporary glass and concrete style. These in turn were partially burnt and badly vandalised, and were demolished in January 1996. They have since been replaced by smaller and simpler waiting shelters. In 2007, the line became part of the London Overground network, passing into the ownership of Transport for London.

Hill's Garage, High Road Leytonstone, in the 1990s. A parade of shops known as the Pavement formerly stood on the site. One of these, Buck's bakery at No. 568 High Road, opened in 1905 and became famous for miles around for its gigantic showpiece Christmas cakes. Hill's Garage developed from the Motor Exchange, run by Cyril and Robert Jackson in the 1950s. Its slogan, 'We never close', was a prominent feature in the High Road until Norman Hill took over the premises. On the opposite side of the High Road is another local legend, Leytonstone Motors. Leytonstone Motors continues to trade today, but ceased to dispense petrol in the 1960s. Hills, however, closed in the late 1990s, presenting an increasingly run-down appearance to the High Road. It was demolished and replaced by flats in the mid-2000s.

Royal Lodge, in the High Road, opposite Davis (or Davies) Lane, c. 1904. This was a very old residence, previously known as Andrews and used as a school until 1821. At the date of the photograph, it had been much modernised, the original building having been largely destroyed by fire in 1878. The grounds originally extended beyond the Midland Railway, and there were some large, extremely old stables, which probably once belonged to the house, that were pulled down when the railway was built. The house was replaced by the Rex (or ABC) cinema, which opened on 21 September 1936. The Rex was a project of Associated British Cinemas and was designed by their in-house architect, William R. Glen. It was the first of the ABC cinemas to use the Rex name and was very posh in an Art Deco way. It had an organ and 1,954 seats and was thought by many to be the classiest cinema in Leytonstone. This is the foyer soon after the cinema's opening.

The Rex cinema had an attractive facade in white tiling, broken by six vertical columns, with two sets of windows between each one. Inside the auditorium, the seating was arranged for 1,174 in the stalls and 780 in the circle. There was a decorative panel in the anti-proscenium side wall on each side which had a woodland tableau depicting deer in a forest. The cinema led an uneventful life and was closed on 18 March 1960. The interior was gutted, with all decoration removed, and at a cost of £100,000 was converted into an ABC tenpin bowling alley, known as the Leytonstone Bowl. It had twenty lanes on two floors – twelve downstairs and eight upstairs. The Leytonstone Bowl was officially opened by the Mayor of Leyton in September 1961. The bowling alley survived for little more than a decade, closing on 20 May 1972. The building became derelict and it was soon demolished, though the site with its huge car park was not redeveloped until the property boom in the 1980s. Blocks of private flats now stand on the site.

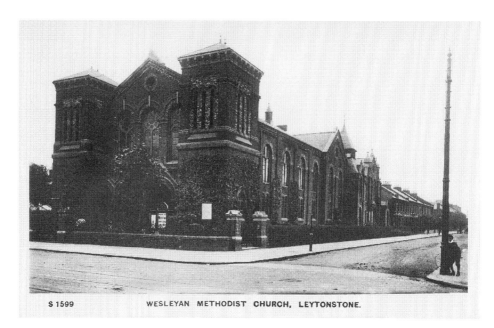

S 1599　　　　　WESLEYAN METHODIST CHURCH, LEYTONSTONE.

Leytonstone Wesleyan Methodist church, at the junction of the High Road and Cowley (now Lister) Road, *c.* 1905. A small iron Wesleyan Methodist chapel, nicknamed the 'Leytonstone Pint Pot' or 'Little Sardine Box', was built on the site in 1876, and a permanent church followed in 1880. This was a brick building with stone dressings and two Italianate west towers. In 1889, the church was enlarged by the addition of a schoolroom, later known as Cowley Hall. It was further enlarged in 1892 and 1902. By 1903, the total Sunday congregations were over 1,000. A memorial hall was built in 1930. The church was demolished in 1968 and a smaller, and much less ornate, modern church now stands on the site.

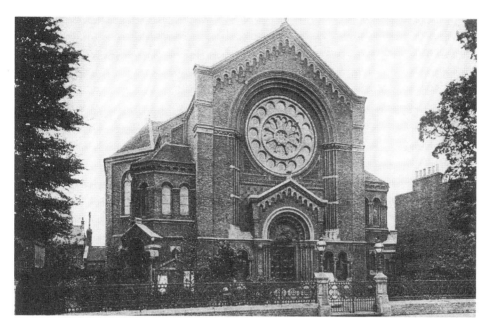

Leytonstone Congregational church, *c.* 1905. A large temporary iron church, capable of holding 400 people, was built in Wellesley Road in 1873 on a site given by William Goodman. The permanent church was built near this iron one in 1877, facing the High Road between Wellesley (now Michael) Road and Barclay Road. It was designed by Lewis Banks, in an elaborate 'Lombardic' style, with seating for 773 people. The church was enlarged in 1888, the seating accommodation increasing to about 1,000. In 1944 the church was damaged by bombing; it was re-opened after repairs in 1946. It was later demolished and, like many buildings in the High Road, was replaced by a block of flats.

The former National School, High Road Leytonstone, *c.* 1890. Leytonstone National schools were founded by 1815. The schools, usually attended by about 100 boys and girls, stood in the yard of the Leytonstone First Chapel of Ease, which stood opposite Barclay Road and was built in 1749. In 1835, the schools were pulled down, the chapel itself converted into schools, and houses built for the master and mistress. Paid monitors were assisting in 1846-47. The schools closed soon after 1876, with the opening of Kirkdale Road School. The building was then used as the local assembly rooms before it was demolished in 1938. An Iceland supermarket, originally Fine Fare, now stands on the site. The building next door opened in the mid-1960s as Leytonstone's main Post Office, but that has since moved to smaller premises, being replaced by a betting shop and a furniture and electrical retailer.

The Red Lion Inn, at the corner of Harvey Road and High Road Leytonstone, *c.* 1885. An inn has stood on this site for many years. The first recorded mention of it is in 1670 when it was the Robin Hood, but by 1766 it had become the Red Lion. As Leytonstone did not have a Town Hall, the Red Lion was frequently used as a meeting and social gathering place – in 1806 a Women's Union Society was meeting at the pub. The weatherboard building in the photograph was demolished in 1890. The ornate replacement inn and shops, designed by W.D. Church, were completed in 1891. There was a period in the 1980s when it was fashionable to change pub names and the pub became Luthers. It later reverted to its traditional (but not its original name), the Red Lion. It has since changed its name again, this time to Zulus, but a red lion is still visible in the decorative stonework above the second-floor windows at the corner.

The *Express and Independent* newspaper offices at the junction of Church Lane and High Road Leytonstone, *c.* 1910. This impressive half-timbered building dated from the mid-1880s. Together with the similarly styled shops further along Church Lane it was pulled down in 1932 for road improvements and the erection of a new Leytonstone public library and electricity showrooms. These were on a new building line set a few feet further back and were opened by the Mayor of Leyton on 8 September 1934. The new library replaced that at Park House by the London, Midland & Scottish Railway (formerly Midland Railway) station further down the High Road. Park House had opened as Leytonstone's first library in 1908. When the new library was opened, Park House was demolished.

Bearmans department store on the day it closed, 23 April 1982. The store was on two sites in the High Road, the one nearer to the Green Man being the furniture department. A new entrance to the main store was built in Kirkdale Road in the 1930s. When Bearmans closed, it was the end of an era. Both buildings were subsequently demolished. A Co-op supermarket opened on the main site, which in turn closed shortly after a large Tesco superstore opened further up the High Road in 2000. The site now houses a Matalan clothes store, a flower shop and a funeral director. Although Bearmans has long been closed, there is still a Bearmans advertisement on the wall in the subway at Leytonstone underground station, near the Church Lane end. When the subway was refurbished in the late 1990s, the advertisement was painted over, to much protest. It has since been uncovered and is now protected behind a plastic shield.

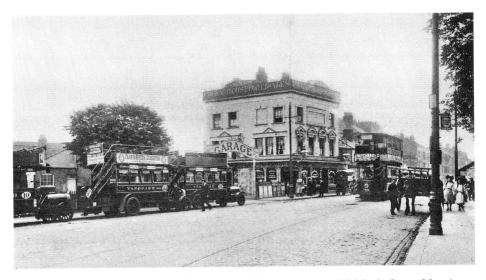

The Green Man inn, at the top of High Road Leytonstone, *c.* 1910. A Green Man inn has been recorded as existing at the point where Leytonstone High Road meets Epping Forest since 1668. The present inn, with its unusual chimneys, is the third and was built in 1927. Its predecessor stood slightly to the south. The second pub was demolished when the new one opened, and for a long time the site was a builders' merchants. A new building was later built on the site as the headquarters of the National Union of Marine, Aviation & Shipping Transport Officers, now Nautilus UK. By the early 1990s, the Green Man inn had been renamed Cubes; it has since become O'Neills, an Irish theme pub. The nearby roundabout, however, continues to bear the name Green Man Interchange. On the opposite side of the High Road, behind the trees, was the Sycamores, a house built in the eighteenth century. It was demolished in 1958 and Leytonstone's Presbyterian Church of Wales now occupies the site. The late-seventeenth century house standing sideways on to the road is home to Musgrave's funeral directors and is Leytonstone's oldest surviving building.

Leytonstone House, August 1999. At the north end of the High Road, Leytonstone House was built *c.* 1800 and was the home of Sir Edward North Buxton, friend of William Wilberforce. From 1847, Thomas Fowell Buxton (son of the liberal reformer of the same name, and Chairman of the Truman, Hanbury & Buxton brewery) and his family lived there when the house was vacated by his elder brother. Ellen Buxton, daughter of Thomas Fowell Buxton (Jnr), kept a diary of her childhood at Leytonstone House in the years 1860-66. These were published by Ellen's granddaughter in the 1960s and provide a fascinating insight into well-off Leytonstone family life immediately before the impact of the railway in the area. In 1868 the Bethnal Green Union Industrial School was established at Leytonstone House by the Bethnal Green poor-law guardians. It closed in 1936 and the buildings subsequently became part of Leytonstone Hospital. That in turn closed in the 1990s, and much of the site is now a large Tesco superstore and car park. Leytonstone House survives as offices, with housing in the remaining school and hospital buildings, and it is now a listed building.

The Green Man pond, c. 1905. This lay at the junction of Bush Road and High Road Leytonstone, and was one of the many gravel pits in this area which became ponds. The pond was a convenient watering hole in an age of horse transport. It was bordered by several large houses, one of which, Ivy Bank, was owned by George Andrew Hutchison, editor of the *Boy's Own Paper*. He lived at Ivy Bank until his death in 1913, and the building later became the Hutchison House Babies' Home for babies born to single mothers. Bushwood House, a large old house possessing very fine marble mantelpieces and attractive grounds, also overlooked the pond. In 1929, Lovetts Garage was erected between the new Green Man pub and the Green Man pond. This survived the Second World War, but was replaced by the John Drinkwater tower block in the 1960s on the site of Bushwood House and Hutchison House. Shortly after the Second World War, the Green Man pond was drained and landscaped into public gardens. The gardens were later remodelled and reopened in July 2006. They are now named after Alderman Henry Reynolds JP.

4

CHURCH LANE

Church Lane in 1876. Church Lane is the link from High Road Leytonstone to the former Great Eastern Railway station, which is just out of sight in the background. Among the private houses on the left is a shop selling tea and coffee. This is reminiscent of a village scene, but when Church Lane was widened in 1884, all the buildings here were demolished.

St John the Baptist church, Leytonstone, *c.* 1905. St John's was built in 1832-33 to the designs of the architect Edward Blore (most notable for his completion of John Nash's design of Buckingham Palace). It replaced a chapel of ease, which became the National School. The church had its own ecclesiastical parish assigned to it on 3 February 1845. St John's was built largely through the enthusiasm of William Cotton, the bank director who lies in its grounds. Its first vicar was a friend of David Livingstone, who came to stay with him on the eve of his journey to Africa. Additions were made to the church in 1893, 1910 and 1929 to cater for the growing population. In 1956, the church was restored and it is now a listed building. A vicarage was built adjacent to the church in the 1850s and continued in use until 1894 when it was sold and a new and more commodious vicarage was built facing Bushwood. Bearmans department store was built on the site of the original vicarage.

Church Lane, looking towards High Road Leytonstone, *c.* 1880. In 1878 a fire engine house was built in Church Lane, adjacent to St John's churchyard. The fire engine station doors are on the left of the picture. In 1902, Leyton Council began widening and rounding off the south-eastern end of Church Lane by setting back the railings of the churchyard. Part of the old fire engine house was allowed to remain, and was adapted to contain the council's electrical transformer. In 1884, Church Lane was widened and everything on the right-hand side of the photograph was demolished to be replaced by impressive half-timbered shops and newspaper offices. They in turn were replaced in 1934 by a more modern building housing Leytonstone's library on the first floor and shops below. The new building also housed a Woolworths store, but this closed, along with all the others nationwide, in January 2009.

Church Lane, Leytonstone, from outside the Great Eastern Railway station, *c.* 1920. When the Eastern Counties Railway (later the Great Eastern Railway) arrived in Leytonstone, Church Lane became the site of a level crossing as the road continued into Fairlop Road. Leytonstone station originally had platforms staggered on each side of the level crossing. In 1907 a fine new parade of shops was opened opposite the station and survives today as Station Parade. The single-storey building on the left at the bend in the road was the Gaiety cinema. This was built in 1888 as the Leytonstone Postmen's Office and it opened as a cinema in 1913 (soon after the office transferred to its new home in Fillebrook Road). It closed in 1928 and was demolished in 1932. It occupied the site at the junction of Kirkdale Road and Church Lane where the Independent Buildings now are. In 1934, it was replaced by shops and new offices for the local *Independent* newspaper, whose offices at the corner of Church Lane and Leytonstone High Road had been demolished for the new Leytonstone Library.

Leytonstone's Great Eastern Railway station, *c.* 1905. On 22 August 1856, the Eastern Counties Railway opened a branch line from Stratford to Woodford and Loughton with a station at Leytonstone. The Great Eastern Railway took over the line in 1862. With the subsequent growth in residential traffic, the Great Eastern rebuilt and made improvements to the station; 1891-92 saw the end of the staggered platforms and included a new public pedestrian subway under the tracks. Between 1882 and 1902, season ticket issues at Leyton and Leytonstone increased by 303 per cent, including a notable 171 per cent growth in first class seasons. However, by 1911, the railway was issuing cheap workmen's tickets from the two stations on the grounds that the areas served were similar in character to that around Maryland Point on the company's main line, where workmen's tickets had always been available.

Work on extending the Central Line to Leytonstone and beyond progressed rapidly, but in May 1940 all work was suspended. The works included the complete rebuilding of Leytonstone station, but for much of the war the station was left in a half-rebuilt state. Electric tube trains finally reached Leytonstone on 5 May 1947. The tube trains terminated in the main up and down platforms at Leytonstone, while steam shuttle services onwards to Loughton, Epping and Ongar ran from the single outer platform. The next advance came on 14 December 1947 when Central Line services were extended from Leytonstone to Woodford and through new tunnels to Newbury Park. Goods trains continued to run on the line at night when tube trains were not running, but these were eventually withdrawn and Leytonstone goods yard closed on 2 September 1955. Some passenger workings were also still operated each way between Epping/Loughton and Liverpool Street/Stratford. Run for the convenience of railway workers, these trains were available to the public, running outside tube traffic hours until finally withdrawn on 31 May 1970. The first photograph shows one such train running early on a Sunday morning in the 1950s; the second shows its counterpart fifty years or so later.

Leytonstone's roller-skating rink, *c.* 1910. The roller-skating rink was opened in October 1907 and was situated in Kirkdale Road behind Bearmans department store. The rink did not last long, however, and on 15 June 1911 it reopened as the Rink Picture Palace with a seating capacity of 1,000, all on one floor. That cinema closed on 30 October 1926 and was bought by the Bernstein chain, who transformed it into the Rialto cinema. The seating capacity was increased to 1,760, with a standing area down the side, stage facilities, a cinema orchestra and a Compton organ. It re-opened as the Rialto on 6 January 1927. The main entrance led down one side of the Bearmans arcade so that film-goers could window-shop in the warm as they queued to get in. In November 1934, the seating capacity was increased to 1,884. It was renamed the Granada cinema from 25 June 1967 and finally closed on 27 April 1974. The cinema was soon demolished and the site was first used as a car park for Bearmans, which was itself demolished in August 1984. A supermarket was built on part of the site, today operating as a Matalan clothes store. Flats have also been built on the Kirkdale Road side of the site. The Compton organ was removed from the cinema in 1973 and is now housed in St Mary's church, Hornchurch, Essex.

Kirkdale Road schools, *c.* 1910. The schools opened in 1876, replacing the nearby National schools. Initially with places for 500 children, by 1891 the school catered for 1,000 children. In 1929, the building was condemned and the seniors and juniors were moved to temporary buildings in Connaught Road. Part of the school was reconstructed and re-opened for infants in 1932; the rest became offices for Leyton Council's education department in 1936. The building was severely damaged by a V2 rocket in 1945, and the school carried on in two classrooms at Connaught Road until it closed in 1948. The education offices were restored and the building survived until the 1970s. The site is now part of the car park for the Matalan store.

Church Lane underpass, Church Lane side, April 1997. Running frequent electric trains to Leytonstone meant that the level crossing between Church Lane and Fairlop Road had to be removed. To enable road traffic to continue to pass from one side of the line to the other, a new road in a cutting with a bridge under the railway was built linking Church Lane with Grove Green Road. The level crossing closed after the war, prior to the electric extension. Work on a new road underpass to replace the level crossing started before the war, but was not completed until after the war. This required demolition of many properties. With the coming of the new A12 (M11 Link Road) in the late 1990s, this underpass was filled in and turned into a car park; the walls at the top of the cutting can still be seen. A new footbridge across the line enables pedestrians to pass from one side to the other.

Church Lane underpass, Grove Green Road side, April 1997. On the Grove Green Road side of the underpass a small playground for children was built on the site of the former dual carriageway. Those wishing to cross the line at the tube station continue to do so in the pedestrian subway there. In honour of the centenary of the birth of film director Alfred Hitchcock (born 13 August 1899 at No. 517 High Road Leytonstone), the London Borough of Waltham Forest commissioned the Greenwich Mural Workshop to create a series of seventeen mosaics of Hitchcock's life and works in the station subway. The work, which started in June 2000, required some 80,000 tiles and took seven months to complete. It was formally unveiled on 3 May 2001. Amongst the scenes from films, there are also images of Leytonstone, portraits of Hitchcock and even trademark cameo roles.

5

FILLEBROOK AND BUSHWOOD

An elaborate 'Swiss Cottage' once stood at the southern edge of Bushwood. This was a timber-framed building dating from about 1850, in a corner of the grounds of Lake House. After the present Lake House estate was built, the cottage remained at the edge of Bushwood and was accessible by a bridge across a ditch or stream. A writer in 1933, recalling childhood events fifty years earlier, noted that '...we made for the avenue at Bushwood, where sometimes there were horse and donkey rides, and swings, not such as you now see, but a rope from a branch of a tree, a board for a seat with a rope hanging down, then with a long pull and a strong pull you went up to the sky. There were stalls for cakes, nuts, toys and ginger beer, and to the garden of Swiss Cottage, hot water at tuppence per head, or teas with watercress for those who could afford it. Some years later I tried to re-visit the place, but found barriers around, with "Trespassers will be prosecuted" facing me there'. The Swiss Cottage was demolished in 1962.

A view down Fairlop Road from outside Leytonstone tube station in about 1960. The buildings on the extreme left were very early post-railway houses, appearing on the Ordnance Survey 25ins to one mile First Edition map, surveyed in 1861–76. However, the pace of development was not always fast. A local historian writing in 1904 noted that, 'Even well within the recollection of the present writer, Fairlop Road was scarcely worthy of the name of a road at all, being of a most primitive character, with a mere sprinkling of houses at the Leytonstone end, and the rest only fields'. By the 1960s, these houses had become part of a motor repair garage. They were demolished thirty years later when the A12 (M11 Link Road) was built through the area. The modern photograph shows that the top end of Fairlop Road has now been incorporated into a small bus station – the Link Road passes underneath in a short tunnel – with buses departing to Hackney, Walthamstow, Woodford and Ilford.

Fillebrook Baptist church, *c.* 1910. This church on the corner of Fairlop Road and Wallwood Road originated in 1874 when drawing-room meetings were held on the initiative of G.A. Hutchison, founder of the *Boy's Own Paper* and local resident. After George Loosley gave a site on the Fillebrook estate, and the London Baptist Association gave £1,000 towards a building fund, a permanent church was opened in 1878. Fillebrook was associated with every kind of social and philanthropic work, including temperance. A hall was built in 1882 and the church enlarged in 1888. A striking new United Free Church building now stands on the site. Next to the church, in Wallwood Road, was Elson House School. This opened as a girls' private school in 1884. In 1905, there were 180 pupils. In 1909-10 the school was amalgamated with the new Leyton County High School for Girls, which opened in Colworth Road in 1911. Elson House preparatory department continued as a private school until 1967, when it was compulsorily closed. There are now flats on the site.

Looking north-east along Fillebrook Road, from the corner of Queens Road, in about 1910 and then again about fifty years later. Fillebrook Road was one of the first roads laid out to the west of the newly arrived railway. Development began when Charles Sansom, inheritor of Wallwood Farm, embarked on a plan to use his land as a building estate, initially to be known as 'Sansomville', but subsequently known as the Fillebrook estate. By 1860, large brick houses had appeared in Fillebrook Road backing onto the railway. Some of this early post-railway housing is on the right. The large houses were empty and derelict by the 1960s, but they survived for a further thirty years before being demolished in the 1990s. The original plan for the estate was to have very large houses like those in the photographs, but this was not a success, with only a handful being sold and the rest had to be let. Less ambitious plans were then drawn up and smaller, but still impressively substantial, houses considered. Progress was slow, however, and for a long time much of the central area was not built on, but let for grazing or for nursery gardens.

Looking north-east from the same location in 1992 and 2008. The earlier photograph shows demolition underway in preparation for the building of the new A12 (M11 Link Road). The saga of the Link Road goes back many years. It has had many names and had been under discussion since the 1920s. In 1962, a public inquiry was held into a proposed Eastern Avenue extension running from the George at Wanstead to Hackney Wick. This would include a new road alongside the Central Line through Leytonstone to Leyton. The then Minister of Transport approved the line orders for the new road and the Department of Transport subsequently bought up much of the property along the route, which then lay derelict for decades. The scheme underwent several more public inquiries and challenges through to the 1990s, before finally opening to traffic in 1999. This section of Fillebrook Road has now been renamed as part of Grove Green Road and Kingswood Road. The modern photograph shows where these roads now meet a realigned Gainsborough Road. The A12 passes under the bridge in the centre of the photograph.

Gainsborough Road, looking towards the Leytonstone Primitive Methodist church in the early 1960s. Leytonstone Primitive Methodist church was sited at the junction of Gainsborough Road, Fillebrook Road, Wallwood Road and Colworth Road. It originated in 1901 when C. Hallam, minister of Stepney Green Tabernacle, held services in Colworth Road for new residents of the Wallwood Park Estate. A permanent church, designed by Hallam, was opened in 1902. It was a two-storey building in the Italian baroque style, consisting of white brick with terracotta dressings; these were mostly replaced by concrete when the west wall was rebuilt after damage in the Second World War. The original turret over the roof became unsafe and was removed in 1930. The building survives today as the Pentecostal City Mission church. Gainsborough Road has now been diverted to accommodate the A12 (M11 Link Road). A footbridge crosses the A12 on the course of the old Gainsborough Road.

Wallwood House, *c.* 1890. Wallwood House stood where Chadwick Road now is. The house in the photograph was the third Wallwood House and was built in 1817–18 to the designs of John Walters for William Cotton, Governor of the Bank of England. In 1894, the house was bought by Thomas Ashbridge Smith who retained only about five acres of the grounds, the remainder being covered with new roads and buildings forming the Wallwood Park estate. During the early years of the twentieth century the estate was completed, leaving only the house and its remaining grounds. Smith occupied Wallwood House until about 1921; the house was demolished shortly afterwards and some distinctive and individual houses were built in its place in Chadwick Road, Ashbridge Road and Whipps Cross Road. The modern view is looking down Chadwick Road, with Victorian houses in the distance on the Wallwood Park estate and more recent houses nearer the camera on the site of Wallwood House.

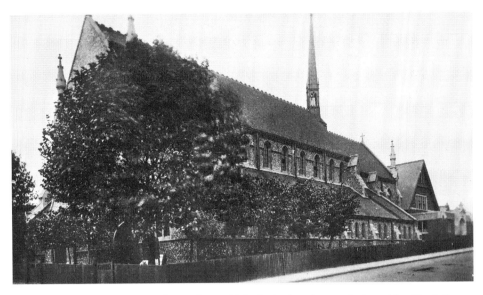

St Andrew's church, Colworth Road, *c.* 1910. St Andrew's was designed by Sir Arthur Blomfield in the Early English style. Building began when the foundation stone was laid by Prince Arthur, Duke of Connaught, on 18 June 1886, with completion in 1892. While steps were being taken towards construction, services (commencing in 1880) were conducted by the clergy of St John's in an iron building in Colworth Road on a site donated by Sir Henry Cotton, son of William Cotton. Around the corner, in St Andrews Road, stood the church hall. This was erected in 1904 and enlarged in 1912. This red brick and stone building was designed in a similar 'Arts and Crafts' style to the nearby Leytonstone School and replaced an earlier Sunday school building. In 1977, the church hall was sold. It later burnt down and the site is now occupied by flats. The streets around the church are a conservation area, and the church itself became a listed building in 2006.

COUNTY HIGH SCHOOL FOR GIRLS, LEYTONSTONE.

Leyton County High School for Girls, Colworth Road, *c.* 1920. Adjacent to St Andrew's church stands Leytonstone School, formerly the Leyton County High School for Girls. The school stands on the site of Forest Farm and opened in 1911. It was designed by W. Jacques in a red brick, seventeenth-century domestic style. It includes numerous features of that age, including a panelled hall with hammerbeam roof. The first headmistress was the founder of the nearby Elson House School, which in 1909-10 amalgamated with the new High School. A new wing was opened in 1932, followed by a swimming pool, for which the school itself raised the money, in 1933. Further extensions were completed in 1957. The school is now Leytonstone Business & Enterprise Specialist School.

Hartley Road at the junction with Beacontree Road, looking north to the John Drinkwater tower block in the early 1990s. On the eastern side of the Great Eastern Railway line, the district between Mornington Road and High Road Leytonstone was being laid out for housing by 1867; development followed with a few cottages in the late 1860s and many small terraced houses in the 1870s and 1880s. Hartley Road was developed as part of the neighbouring Leyspring estate laid out over the next twenty years. The John Drinkwater tower block (named after the poet, who was born in Leytonstone in 1882) was erected in the 1960s behind the Green Man inn. Like many similar high-rise buildings, it fell out of favour. It was demolished in 1998 and replaced by low-rise housing. The poet's name survives, however, in John Drinkwater Road.

Bushwood Road, *c.* 1910. Bushwood (which has dropped the 'Road' part of its name) looks onto the fringes of Epping Forest. It was developed as part of the Leyspring estate on the site of Leyspring House. This was a fine house, with a spring in the courtyard and very extensive grounds covering over thirty-three acres. The grounds were bounded on the north by Park Road (now Browning Road) and on the south and east by Bushwood; on the west it extended nearly to Mornington Road. The house was occupied in the mid-nineteenth century by Nicholas Charrington, the founder of the well-known brewery. Leyspring House was destroyed by fire in about 1870 and the estate was redeveloped with roads and houses. In the hundred years or so between the two photographs, the trees on the right have grown considerably larger.

Bushwood avenue, *c.* 1910. Sir Josiah Child, merchant banker and head of the East India Company, purchased the manor of Wanstead in 1667 and on his instructions had planted avenues of Spanish chestnuts in quincunx formation, radiating from his nearby home, Wanstead House. The grandest were the three avenues through what is now Blake Hall Road to Leytonstone. Nearly 350 years later, the avenue still stands out clearly. The rustic footbridge visible through the trees in the earlier photograph crossed a ditch and led to Leytonstone's 'Swiss Cottage'. The cottage was demolished in 1962, in spite of local protests, when the Metropolitan Police erected a multi-storey accommodation block for police cadets on the site. This is now a residential development called Belgrave Heights and stands out above the trees.

Leytonstone Keeper's Cottage, Bushwood

Bushwood in Leytonstone lies at the southern end of Epping Forest. This is the largest public open space in the London area, at almost 6,000 acres. It stretches twelve miles from Manor Park to beyond Epping in Essex. As well as being a popular area for recreation, it is also of national and international conservation importance. In the second half of the nineteenth century, large areas of the forest were being enclosed for development, with little regard for commoners' rights to graze their animals and cut wood. Such was the City of London's concern over this that it joined forces with the commoners and fought a legal battle against the enclosures, culminating in the Epping Forest Act of 1878, which appointed the City of London as the Conservator of Epping Forest. Its strictures still govern how the forest is managed today. A forest keeper's cottage has stood at Bushwood for more than a century.

Bush Road & Park Gates — Leytonstone

Photo by C. E. Webber. Published by E. T. Walker, Stationer Leytonstone

Bush Road, Leytonstone, *c.* 1905. The two Portland stone pillars stand each side of the Bush Gate, now one end of Overton Drive, and are the original piers of the carriageway to Wanstead House (demolished in 1822). They bear the interlaced monogram of Sir Josiah Child. To the right of the entrance stands Park House, the residence of Sir (later Lord) John Henry Bethell, Liberal MP for Romford. In 1931 it was converted into flats, but bomb damage in 1941 resulted in its subsequent demolition. On the left was Park Gate, the home of Alderman Sir Thomas Finnis, the last Lord Mayor of London (1856-57) to have his procession on the Thames. It was demolished in the early twentieth century for the building of the Blake Hall estate. The piers are listed buildings, and the balls on top were added when the right-hand pillar was repaired by the local council.

6

WHIPPS CROSS

The High Stone, on the border between Leytonstone and Wanstead, *c.* 1925. This was the spot where Leyton was created a Municipal Borough on 2 October 1926. The High Stone was allegedly set up by Roman soldiers as a landmark, boundary or milestone and stands at the junction of Woodford Road (now Hollybush Hill) and New Wanstead, just to the north of where Whipps Cross Road used to meet Woodford Road. The 8ft-high obelisk is of nineteenth-century origin, but the base is said to be part of the original. Made of Portland stone, and now a listed building, the obelisk's well worn (almost invisible) inscription in lead lettering states, 'The base of this stone formed part of the original high stone' and gives the distance to Epping as 'XI miles'; Epping to Ongar through Woodford Bridge, Chigwell and Abridge as 'XV miles'; and that to Hyde Park Corner as what appears to be '10 miles'.

The southern end of Whipps Cross Road, where it was joined by Woodford Road,
c. 1910. A Leyton tram heads for Whipps Cross then Clapton, having already called at
Stratford and Leytonstone. Leyton's trams sported a dark green and primrose livery,
with Leyton District Council Tramways in gold lettering on the side. This road junction
disappeared in the early 1960s when the first Green Man roundabout was constructed,
replacing what had by then become a free-for-all junction of intersecting roads. In the
1990s, there was more upheaval as the roundabout was reconstructed as part of the
A12 (M11 Link Road) route. At the new interchange the Link Road is in a tunnel with
a new and bigger roundabout with extensive and improved provision for pedestrians,
cyclist and horses above.

LEYTON, WHIPP'S CROSS ROAD. 73377

Whipps Cross supposedly gains its name from having been the starting point from which those who were found stealing wood or deer from Epping Forest were whipped at the cart-tail. Be that as it may, the area with its large open spaces has long been an area for fun and recreation. Writers in the early twentieth century reported that, come Saturday and Sunday, there was always something going on at Whipps Cross, with itinerant entertainers galore, and a brass band on Sunday mornings. Whipps Cross Road runs from the Green Man through to Whipps Cross at the top of Lea Bridge Road. This view from the 1930s shows a motor bus and a tram passing, while the cyclist in the foreground tries not to get his wheels stuck in the tram lines.

A tramway opened along Whipps Cross Road in 1906. The original tram tracks were positioned in the carriageway. During the early 1920s improvements to the layout resulted in a reserved double track on the north side of the road. The wiring on this section was suspended from poles on one side of the track only, rather than on both sides as elsewhere. This halved the amount of money ('wayleave payments') due to the Conservators of Epping Forest for the total number of poles on their land. The almost straight run of one and a quarter miles from the Green Man to Whipps Cross on the reserved track was a delight for tram drivers; if a passenger had the temerity to ring the bell en route, the driver was almost annoyed and considered himself done out of something. A London Transport tram hurries along the reserved track in the 1930s. Seventy-five years later, the distinctive tree helps locate the same spot.

A horse tramway had reached Whipps Cross via Lea Bridge Road in 1883. This was electrified and opened under the ownership of Leyton Council in 1906. In July 1921, Leyton Council opted for an arrangement with the London County Council whereby the larger operator undertook to supply and repair rolling stock. Leyton's network was transferred to the new London Transport Board in 1933, and in the photograph two ex-Leyton trams in London Transport red and cream livery stand at Whipps Cross. Whipps Cross continues to be a busy traffic intersection and a terminus for some buses.

A trolleybus on route 581 to Bloomsbury negotiates Whipps Cross roundabout in the 1950s. The process of replacing Leyton's trams with trolleybuses began in October 1936 and the local tram tracks finally fell silent with the conversion of tram route 61 to trolleybus 661 on 5 November 1939. As the trolleybus scheme took hold, so new traffic arrangements like the construction of a roundabout at Whipps Cross became necessary for providing turning circles for the new vehicles. The trolleybuses were in turn superseded by motor buses, route 661 being replaced by bus route 26, and by April 1960 all local trolleybus services had been replaced.

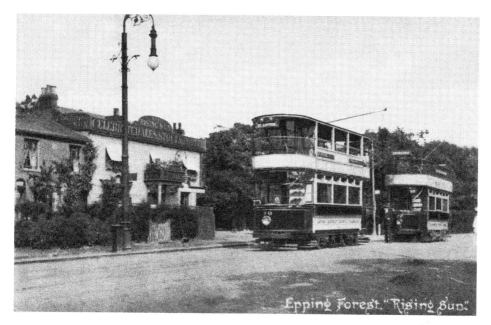

The Rising Sun public house, *c.* 1910. The Rising Sun on Woodford New Road was where two tram lines met, but with no physical connection between them. By 1892, horse trams belonging to the Lea Bridge, Leyton & Walthamstow Tramways Company were traversing tracks from Upper Clapton to the Rising Sun, and from 1 December 1906 Leyton's electric trams replaced these. Walthamstow Council also ran a service to the Rising Sun from Waterworks Corner/Forest Road, but this was poorly patronised. In fact, Leyton's services to the Rising Sun ran only spasmodically, sometimes only on Sundays, for trippers from less salubrious surroundings to enjoy the delights and cleaner air of Epping Forest. The Rising Sun inn was built in 1846, enlarged in 1850 and modernised in the 1960s. It was largely rebuilt in 2008 when it was renamed the RS Lounge.

James Lane, *c.* 1905. This view shows the east side of James Lane, with a tea-house and St Andrew's church visible in the background through the trees. The trees in the centre have thick branches sawn short high up, perhaps to provide more light to the ground in front of the tea-house. Small cottage tea-gardens were a type of business common in the Epping Forest area. Generally they supplied a pot of tea, bread and butter, watercress in season, jam and slices of fruit or plain cake or rock cakes for a modest sum. The seating in the garden was on rustic-style benches placed at similar tables. A tablecloth covered the table. Several tea gardens were happy to supply a pot of tea to accompany the packed meal brought by the visitor, or even to supply boiling water for the party to brew their own tea. Should the weather turn wet, the cottager would either accommodate the visitors in shed-like structures or within the cottage.

Looking down James Lane, *c.* 1910. James Lane runs from Whipps Cross Road to High Road Leyton and is recorded as far back as 1484. It formed one of the boundaries to the Forest House estate. This view looks past the entrance to Forest House on the right, with the duck pond clearly visible alongside. Behind the brick wall further down the road were numerous glasshouses serving Forest House. These have long gone and Whipps Cross hospital's ambulance station now stands there.

Forest House in the 1890s. Forest House dated from 1683 and was the residence of Lord Goring, Earl of Norwich, in the seventeenth century. In 1889, Forest House was purchased as an annexe to the West Ham Union workhouse at Langthorne for 300 aged men, and in 1903 an infirmary opened in the grounds. This grew into today's Whipps Cross Hospital. Forest House was offered to the War Office in 1915 for war wounded, but this was not taken up until October 1917 when a war hospital opened catering for 180 acute and 160 convalescent patients in the annexe and part of the infirmary. Forest House subsequently became an old people's home, being closed in 1962 when a new hostel, Samuel Boyce Lodge, was opened in the grounds. Despite becoming a listed building in 1953, it was demolished in 1964. A portakabin and car park are now on the site.

The main entrance to Whipps Cross Infirmary, *c.* 1905. In 1889, the West Ham Union guardians of the poor had bought Forest House with its forty-four acre estate, and in 1895 approved plans for a new infirmary there. When opened in 1903, the infirmary had 672 beds in twenty-four wards housed in four blocks, and was one of the first large-scale Poor Law infirmaries in the London area. In 1917, the name of the infirmary was changed to Whipps Cross Hospital and administration passed to West Ham Council, the guardians noting that it 'was coming to be regarded by the public more of a general hospital than an infirmary', the latter term having hated workhouse connections. In later years, Graham Gooch (cricketer), Jonathan Ross (television presenter) and David Beckham (footballer) were all born at Whipps Cross Hospital. The hospital is recognised as a training school and now bears the name Whipps Cross University Hospital.

Whipps Cross lake, or the Hollow Ponds, *c.* 1910. The Hollow Ponds are a legacy of the nineteenth-century demand for gravel for road building, when the ponds were excavated to provide unemployment relief work. Some gravel was sold, but much was just piled up. After the Epping Forest Act of 1878, the pools were enlarged by the Conservators of Epping Forest for recreational use. A large ornamental pond on swampy ground was constructed between 1897 and 1901 when it was reported by Leyton Council that, 'The formation of this pond, with islands and sloping banks, has much improved the appearance of that part of the Forest, and provided facilities for swimming, boating and model yacht sailing; and the depth being very shallow, it is a safe place for skating'. The Hollow Ponds really came into their own when frozen in a cold winter, when roast chestnuts and toffee apples were sold there and skates were available for hire. The Hollow Ponds have been a magnet for children and adults for more than 100 years and they are still popular for fishing, walking and boating.

Whipps Cross Lido in the 1950s. The lido evolved from one of the Hollow Ponds dug by the unemployed. It was fed by natural springs and soon became muddy and unhygienic so, in 1923, improvements were made including levelling and cleansing the bottom and lining it with concrete. By 1932, four large dressing rooms were provided and the surround was paved. Further work followed to convert the lake into a modern, chemically treated and filtered lido, which opened in 1937. Of the thirty-five open-air swimming pools constructed in London in the 1930s, this was the largest: 300ft long and 130ft wide, a depth range of 3ft 6ins – 5ft 6ins, and a capacity of 1.3 million gallons. There was also a unique 63ft diameter and 10ft deep circular diving basin to the south-west, but connected to the main section. At the north-eastern end were changing rooms and a fountain. By 1981, however, attendance had fallen to under 20,000 per year, and the lido closed on 4 September 1982. It was quickly filled in by the Corporation of the City of London, the buildings demolished and the land reforested by December 1983. Only the approach road, some broken pipes, and the embankments remain visible today.

Other titles published by The History Press

London Past and Present
MICHAEL BARRETT

Using a selection of images from *London in the Postwar Years* by Douglas Whitworth, Michael Barrett compares them with modern views taken from identical positions. The images are accompanied by captions explaining the changes which have occurred. Michael Barrett's stunning colour photography contrasts with the evocative views of the post-war years to create an important visual record of England's capital city.

978 0 7524 4304 1

Haunted London Pubs
DAVID BRANDON AND ALAN BROOKE

This book reports the many stories of ghostly sightings at London's drinking places, and delves into the fascinating history surrounding them. From the ghosts of prisoners still trying to escape the nearby Millbank Prison through tunnels under the Morpeth Arms, to the chilling spectre of the screaming girl at The Horns in Crucifix Lane, this book is a creepy must-read for anyone interested in the haunted history of London's pubs.

978 0 7524 4760 5

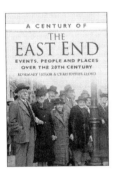

A Century of the East End
ROSEMARY TAYLOR AND CHRIS LLOYD

This fine selection of photographs illustrates the transformation that has taken place in the East End during the twentieth century, offering insight into the daily lives and living conditions of local people during a century of change. Illustrated with a wealth of black-and-white photographs, it acknowledges the regeneration that has taken place and celebrates the character and energy of local people.

978 0 7509 4912 5

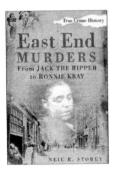

East End Murders: From Jack the Ripper to Ronnie Kray
NEIL R. STOREY

Neil R. Storey has drawn on a vast array of original sources – among them witness statements, coroners' reports and court records – to produce a revealing insight into the East End's darkest moments. As well as the murders of Jack the Ripper, perhaps the most infamous in history, he looks at nine other cases in detail.

978 0 7509 5069 5

Visit our website and discover thousands of other History Press books.
www.thehistorypress.co.uk

Printed in Great Britain
by Amazon